P9-CEO-496

ILLINOIS CENTRAL COLLEGE
PS647.S4L4
STACKS
Journeys;
A12900 245006

BOOKS BY RICHARD LEWIS

Journeys
Muse of the Round Sky
Still Waters of the Air
Of This World
The Park
The Wind and the Rain
Out of the Earth I Sing
Moon For What Do You Wait?
Miracles
In a Spring Garden
The Moment of Wonder
In Praise of Music

JOURNEYS

Prose by Children of the English-Speaking World

collected by

RICHARD LEWIS

SIMON AND SCHUSTER • NEW YORK

ACKNOWLEDGMENTS

The editor would like to thank Mr. L. A. Minnich and Miss Carol Olson of the U.S. National Commission for Unesco as well as the various personnel of the Unesco Commissions of the United Kingdom, Canada, New Zealand, Australia, India, Liberia and Ghana for their generous cooperation and assistance in the preparation of this book. My gratitude to the many parents, teachers and school administrators who aided me in my search for material; to Miss Jane Lippe for her excellent typing of the manuscript; to my wife Nancy for her devotion and concern; to my editor, Richard Locke, whose wisdom and editorial skill are such an integral part of this book; and my wholehearted thanks to the children who have made it all possible.

Every care has been taken to trace the ownership of every selection included and to make full acknowledgment for its use. If any errors have accidentally occurred, they will be corrected in subsequent editions, provided notification is sent to the publisher.

[*Acknowledgments continued on page 214*]

Published by Simon and Schuster
Rockefeller Center, 630 Fifth Avenue, New York, N.Y. 10020

FIRST PRINTING

SBN 671-20364-9 Trade
SBN 671-65088-2 Library
Library of Congress Catalog Card Number: 70-87882
Designed by Helen Barrow
Manufactured in the United States of America

To the Children

CONTENTS

INTRODUCTORY NOTE

Journeys *is a collection of prose by children. It is intended as a companion volume to my anthology of poetry,* Miracles. *The children whose work is represented here come from different backgrounds and write from different impulses, but all of them have created some kind of prose that reflects their own experience. Whether story or description, character study or essay, or any of the other types of prose, their work can be read as literature, not merely as a curiosity.*

This book had its beginnings in 1961 in the classes in writing and literature that I taught in an elementary school in New York. During that year I began to see that if children were allowed to write in whatever form they wished, they had much to say about themselves and their world. When left alone with paper and pencil their responses to language as an expressive medium were always highly individual. Some would write poetry, some would write stories, some just a paragraph and others no more than a sentence. Their decision to write poetry or prose or a cross between the two usually was governed by no more than their desire to express something important to them in their own personal style. They seldom began with a literary form and then searched for an appropriate subject to fit it. Their choice of subject and the internal logic of their responses to it determined the shape of what each child eventually wrote. Because so much of their work took shape as prose, it seemed clear that a companion volume to Miracles *would be needed to show the entire scope of children's capacity to create literature.*

I was especially fortunate when making this collection to have had once more the generous cooperation of the United

States National Commission for UNESCO and the various UNESCO commissions throughout the English-speaking world that helped me supplement prose material I had gathered on my world tour to collect children's poetry in 1964. Again material came from schools, parents, and children themselves, in some eighteen countries where English is the native language or an important secondary language.

As I read the children's writing and made selections, certain types of prose seemed consistently more successful than others. It was clear that shorter prose worked better than longer prose, in which the language tended to lose the energy that comes from fresh concentration. Narratives generally tended to falter, except when the first person was used. Simple declarative statements that often had the sharp ring of poetry tended to be more successful as prose than were attempts at sustained, objective discussions of set themes. In short, whenever a child could write out his own freely chosen experiences, thoughts, feelings and fantasies, creating a form and idiom entirely his own—it was then that a truly exciting piece of prose emerged.

All of the prose in this book is exactly as the children intended it. The only corrections made have been in spelling and in capitalizing words at the beginning of sentences.

It is my hope that this collection will demonstrate the imaginative and expressive power of children when they are encouraged to write in their own ways of themselves and of things important to them. The children ask only that we read their work as they wrote it—carefully, seriously, openly —so that we can discover with them the experience of the journeys that are their lives.

—R.L.

MARCH 1969

What I want to write about. Everything.

Anonymous AGE 10 UNITED STATES

ONE

Beginnings

THE SUN

The Sun sees everything. In the old days they thought the Sun had a chariot, but you and I know that they were wrong and that the Sun just sits there and makes sure the planets don't go off course. He rose to power with kindness, being cheerful, and when it was necessary to let the clouds come and bring good life-giving rain. Soon everyone respected the Sun and he was made King of All Nature, with old Mother Nature herself the Queen.

Kevin Canty AGE 9 UNITED STATES

CREATION

The earth voomed out like a baseball.

Adam Sternglass AGE 8 UNITED STATES

They all started to dance away. The bird danced so high he flew out of the sky as the North Star. The cat danced so much that he became a part of the big dipper. The same thing happened with the rest of the people. They formed the big dipper. The music spread all over the world. Everyone danced into the sky as stars. Just then the big dipper that the animals made poured violins, flutes, pianos and a whole orchestra. The music took over the world. Everyone was making the music louder. It came more and more delightful that mother nature danced making all the trees and flowers. It was unfortunate but just then the trees trampled the people playing the music. The stars danced no longer but were stuck in the sky as stars.

The trees didn't want to trample the musicians but danced. The whole world became sad. The trees and houses fell. Everybody was sad.

But very luckily in a small tree lived a bird. He started to sing a lone tune which made the trees come together but stationary so they couldn't trample the musicians as they came back. The stars twinkled and music, but only music, lived on the earth.

Ernie Rubinstein AGE 9 UNITED STATES

THE SEAHORSE

Once in the lagoons deep in the sea there was a small lonely seahorse. He didn't have any parents so he was very shy. Life at that time was boring for him. He didn't have many friends except for the plants and oysters, but you can't really talk to plants and oysters because they sleep all the time. One day another seahorse came to that part of the sea. She was just like him except she was a girl seahorse. Then all of a sudden they bumped into each other and . . .

Alison Mitchell AGE 10 NEW ZEALAND

THE WEDDING OF FISH AND KENKEY

Once upon a time there lived the fish in the sea. This fish decided to marry. One day the fish came out from the sea—to land. There he saw the kenkey [cornmeal] at the shore of the sea. In fact, as soon as he saw the kenkey, he became happy at seeing the kenkey. So he shouted "Dear friend will you marry me?" The kenkey replied "Oh! Yes. I hope to do so." So the fish took kenkey to Mr. Hot Water and boiled it. From there kenkey also took fish to Mr. Hot Oil, to fry it. Then they all went to Mrs. Plate. In some few days time the kenkey gave birth to pepper. Mrs. Plate decided to give them to Mr. Stomach to keep them for some time. That is why we always see kenkey and fish with pepper in a plate ready for the stomach.

Asare Edward AGE 14 GHANA

MAN EMERGES FROM NATURE

Mother nature had created a beautiful world, with grass, mountains and lakes. But she was not satisfied, she wanted a living creature on the surface of the earth. She thought that a flower would do just fine for a beginning. This is how she went about it. She took a little salt water and sprinkled it over the leaves, so they should grow into hands. Next she took some dew that was lying on the earth, she also sprinkled it over two roots of the flower and they too turned into feet. For the body she split the stem and put a potato inside and sewed it up. Then she took a rain drop from a cloud, sprinkled it on and it also grew bigger. When she got to the face she had a bit of trouble, but she still did not give up. She took a drop of dew again and it made the petals close up to form the oval of the face. She took the fuzz off a peach to make the skin. For the lips she used two red leaves. For the nose she used a carrot. She took two stars from the sky for eyes and the wind blew the loose grass on the head for hair. Man was created!

Maura Copeland AGE 10 UNITED STATES

LOVE

Man sees woman and love comes upon the two. Many years go by and make their own way of love and married love and do what they want to do. They kiss get all and have children and that is how the world began and we are thankful for them.

Tony Ibanez AGE 11 UNITED STATES

The earth is silent for a moment. Then we open our eyes. It is dusty and gloomy, until you suddenly realize that it is a beautiful place.

Anne Prager AGE 9 UNITED STATES

TULIPS

I have painted some tulips. I have painted them red, yellow, black, a tiny bit of white and a green stalk, and a white pistil, and yellow stamens, yellow and red petals, and black pollen. And there is a tiny bit of red on the end of each petal, and there is purple inside of the pollen, and at the bottom of the stalk it looks like bubbles, and it feels like some satin, and it looks like a rainbow, and the petals look like hearts.

Anonymous AGE 6 ENGLAND

SPRING

The breeze, gentle, cool, floats, twisting turning leap-frog playing, glides silent except for the rustling of leaves in the trees above. The crocuses, heads gone, stand, droop, lie on the damp dew-dropped carpet of green.

Trees with new clean fresh leaves growing, silent, but growing all the while. The rhododendron, flowers of a great cluster, single petal, crimson flame, living burning, growing till the yellow, golden brown leaf-falling autumn. The Dandelion clock, time in the tight clamped hand. One, three, five or thirteen o'clock. The Daffodil in its prime, yellow, bright golden yellow.

John Downey AGE 10 IRELAND

CAVE MEN

Once upon a time there was two cave men with brims on their hats, and they went to a little stream to get fish, and one day a typhoon came and the two cave men had to take everything into the cave so it would not get blown away, and they had to live in the cave for ninety-nine years. And when they came out it was sunshining, and they went to the stream to get a drink and some fish, and they caught twenty apiece, and they had forty altogether. And in the light time they would have a swim, and then they would fish for tea, and then they would lie down and go to sleep and dream, and their dreams came true.

Anonymous AGE 7 ENGLAND

TWO

Days

This morning I woke up real late I was *tired.* I looked out the window and I saw nothing but fog and I got my coat on and got my dog and sent him out in the fog and he chewed the paper up and I told my father to go to work and the fog was too thick and he nearly crashed in to the telegraph pole and then I went to take my dog for a walk in the fog and the lead tangled around something and I went round one way and the dog went round the other way and I banged into him and I tripped over him. Then something shined into my face and I looked up for a while and saw the sun breaking through the fog and I started to walk home and got dressed and got dressed again for school and drove to school and I went to the play ground and it was still foggy. Then the sun came out bright.

Brett Cameron AGE 7 AUSTRALIA

ON A FOGGY MORNING

The tops of the trees looked like a bundle of balloons at a standstill.

Karen Saunders AGE 9 AUSTRALIA

I saw the road. It was sitting down. It was brown and rocky.

Philmore Cooper AGE 8 LIBERIA

ROCKS

Hard rocks are prickly and dangerous but soft rocks are smooth and tender. And the best rocks, which are the middle rocks, are only powerful! But all rocks are fainty and faint away when they're very old. Rocks are funny the way they jump up and down and roll around in summersaults, falling from volcanoes.

Alissa Guyer AGE 8 UNITED STATES

WATER

Water is like loose jelly mixed into mud. It tumbles down on the rocks making big booms as it goes down. When it goes down the plughole it sounds like a frog croaking. It crashes in the sea making tremendous waves.

Water sets on the grass like a plate of gold.

Gregory Phillip Elliott AGE 5 NEW ZEALAND

Drops of dew, a thousand silver pennies—floating, slithering down layers of the sky and sun. Then as it hits the earth, dies in silence.

Rick Rothenberg AGE 9 UNITED STATES

QUIET FISHING

My float was silent and still, and its yellow and white markings gleamed in my ever fading eyes. The gentle fall of distant water could be heard as it pounded the stream. My mind went with the water, up and down, in and out, moving forward as it went. You let your mind run away, as if swept away by the stream.

Michael Freeman AGE 11 ENGLAND

Fish are like little petals of a flower moving in the cool spring breeze, tiny and delicate, when someone blows the flower very hard the petals ride briskly along in the breeze.

Gina Roose AGE 9 UNITED STATES

He settled himself down between two rocks, scrabbled with his feet idly in the sand, and surveyed the village. A dog limped behind the man and his white cow as they stumbled through the hot shade at the bottom of the hill, under the trees by the cracking houses. He could see the flies dodging on the cow's back through the heat. The village became further and further away as he stared at it: the trees shimmered in the heat; dust rose in small clouds as the cows kicked their way across the stones.

He was looking down, like a god, from above the trees. He could see the women congregating under one of the trees, with their pitchers; a cow nodded at the edge of the shade, swaying its thick, mottled head. The tufts of grass were running with sweat in the sun. The tufts of grass. He watched a caterpillar scurrying across the sand under one of the clumps. Into the cool, stony unknown. He moved his knee slowly away from the tuft of grass, and sat up. His hair clung to his forehead; he pushed it back, glanced down at the village to see that no one was watching, and crouched by the tuft. A cow came wandering round the outcrop of rock, nosing the sand; it stopped, and watched him. The flies settled on its eyelids.

He squatted down, and tossed a stone at the grass. Nothing stirred. He smiled benevolently at the cow; it shook its head, the flies rose, and settled again. The grass was sweating in the sun.

Richard R. Crook AGE 13 ENGLAND

SUMMER

The world in a glass bowl. The sun a giant flaming ball floating in space. Blue sky like the sea with drifting icebergs. I screw up my face in the sun. When I look up through the trees I see patches of blue and a blearing sun looking through. I listen under the tree and hear the cicadas singing. The breeze under the trees makes the grass shiver.

Alex Moreland AGE 10 NEW ZEALAND

THE DANDELION

PART I: *Before You Blow It*

Before you blow a dandelion, it has about 100 soft, silky bristles. A bristle looks like it has as many shooting out parts as a picture of the sun has rays. It looks sort of like a tiny, tiny snowy tree. Each bristle has a stalk to hold it to the middle. All the bristles put together make a ball sort of shape. There is a brown ball that holds the bristles together and there is a stem. The stem also keeps it from falling apart.

PART II: *While You Blow It*

You see thousands of tiny bristles falling apart because when you blow it, your air makes the bristles come off the brown ball and the stem. If you blow it inside, it gets all over the room. If you blow it outside, it will get all over you, so watch out!

PART III: *After You Blow It*

The dandelion is gone. You blew it apart. Now if you read this story outside while having a picnic, all you have left is the stem and the brown ball and you, covered with dandelion bristles. The stem looks like a thin piece of green celery. The brown ball has a green surface on top, sort of like a hat. It has holes like on a shower nozzle. And that is what you find when you blow a dandelion.

John Thomas Roddey Holder AGE 6 UNITED STATES

A flower feels like feathers. It is smooth, almost furry. It smells like perfume. Its smell is lovely like a garden of flowers. It looks like a two-headed, four-armed giant. If it could sing it would sing I'm a two-headed giant all day long. It would sing deep and masculine.

Amy Schwartz AGE 9 UNITED STATES

MY TREE

My tree is a mass of greenness and tallness and fatness. My tree has jagged leaves and is like an octopus soaking its leaves in the light.

John M. AGE 10 NEW ZEALAND

Class 1 had Monday off and Tuesday off and all the other classes had Monday and Tuesday off and we played hide-and-seek and my big sister hid her eyes and counted up to ten and me and my brother had to hide and I went behind the dustbin and I was thinking about the summer and the buttercups and daisies and all those things and fresh grass and violets and roses and lavender and the twinkling sea and the star in the night and the black sky and the moon.

Sally-Anne Fryman AGE 7 ENGLAND

My pretend friend is Sgt. Saunders and we play Army together. We blast our tommy guns and houses and knock out Kraut machine gun nests. We also smoke. We also go on daring assignments like to find a Kraut O.P. and to be captured and escape. Army life is a hard life.

Harry Schneider AGE 8 UNITED STATES

PLAYING SOCCER

When I was playing soccer I got shoved. I twirled and twisted as I lost my balance. I buckled and bent and folded up like an umbrella. I rolled along the ground. Colors blurred in my eyes, and they mixed into patterns of funny shaped people and peculiar colored houses.

Tommy Waldie AGE 10 NEW ZEALAND

GAINING MY FIRST GOAL

Up, up, up and oh help. Why didn't it go in like it should have? It should go up and in so very perfectly, and it's got to. Up, up, ah, it's going, going, gone. Blast it. I know I'm standing wrongly and yes, um Barbara always says, "The sun's in my eyes." Well, "The sun's in my eyes." But it can't be, I'm inside.

I know, maybe I'm better at long shots. When Barbara takes them she stands nine feet away, and I'm four years younger and one foot smaller, so, four plus one is *six* and nine take away six equals *two*. Therefore I stand two feet away.

Hey, this looks better, just right. Oh, not again it can't miss. But it's not, it's going to go in.

Oh help, aren't I just so good.

Pamela McHenry AGE 12 NEW ZEALAND

One day I went to Porirua on the train. When I got there I was playing in the tunnels when a man came along. He came down some steps and was walking along by a wall when he banged into the wall and hurt himself. He was tall and skinny, he had blacky, brown hair and a blue and white hat, gray trousers and a blue shirt, big dirty boots and green socks. He kept shaking hands with people. Then when I was going on the train home, I saw the man in the same carriage sitting opposite me. He was reading a book about war. What a shame he was reading because he missed all the hills, rivers, trees, and the beautiful birds and butterflies. I had to get off at the next stop and as I was going up the ramp, the last I saw of him, he was dozing over his book.

Hazel Crewe AGE 8 NEW ZEALAND

THE THEATER

The lights stare down, murmuring voices fill the building and people stamp and run around dodging obstacles. There's the spit of a peashooter and howling voices. Eyes look up as the lights go off. Crumpled paper flies through the air. The sweet and mouth-watering smell of aniseed balls creeps up my nose. Children flounder along the rows in the dark hoping that they'll still have their seats. The curtains part and the music plays triumphantly. The seats crash as people rise.

Geoffrey Waghorn AGE 12 NEW ZEALAND

Last year I was watching the cars by my house. They were slippin' around just like tails swishin' on cats.

Brian Hoban AGE 7 UNITED STATES

THE FIRE HYDRANT

It's like a strange plant bursting with its juice. Like a city's waterfall. I wouldn't be surprised if a whale came out today.

Ricky Preiskel AGE 10 UNITED STATES

THE AUTOMOBILES' CRASH-UP

One day there were two autos. They got in a crash. Ambulances came! Fire trucks came! Everybody came running! Women with their babies.

More and more autos crashed. The autos were on the freeway. They caused a forest fire. Everything was on fire! It took all the fire engines in the world to put out the fire.

Everyone wanted to help. They even hooked up hoses to the fire hydrants and used them. The babies watched. One of them got into mischief and turned off one of the sirens of a fire truck.

Michael Klaus AGE 6 UNITED STATES

WHEN I SAW A WRECK

I was walking up the street when a white 1967 Chevy came out from Curtis and a brown 1966 Ford coming from the north end of William. When the brown car started to get where the white car was the white car pulled out. Then the brown car tried to dodge the white car but the brown car lost control and skidded and slid into a telephone pole and swirled into a yard. When the policeman got there he asked me a lot of things about the wreck. My heart felt like it turned over.

Lawther Wood AGE 9 UNITED STATES

Apartment buildings have many eyes. That is a sad thing for they must look at all the evils of man, until they are torn down. Then the mechanical things weep. Weep in their own way. They weep oil. Oil is the sorrow of machines.

Sara Maltz AGE 11 UNITED STATES

FROM MY WINDOW

Tuesday:

I see only two bags of garbage and about 20 pigeons. I see a boy looking out a window. Then the mother comes and tells him to do something. I see that the sky is cloudy and it looks like it's going to rain. I see that a lot of smoke is coming out of our chimney. I see no lights are on and I see pigeons on our window. I see it is not maybe going to be a good day.

Wednesday:

I see garbage and an empty box of Kellogg's corn flakes and two bags full of garbage. I see a red metal tub something in the right side that you pick up garbage with. I also see eleven bars. I see many bricks they look like brick paper. I could see a couple of pigeons plus a big chimney. I see that the sky is getting dark. I hear people talking. I see eleven windows and four have their lights on.

Thursday:

I see it is getting dark and that it is about 7:00 or 7:30 that it looks spooky and I see pigeons going to sleep. I see some on my window that are not singing and that there are around seven lights on and bricks. I see around eleven windows. I also see a boy going to sleep I see a man and a woman seeing TV and that they are seeing "Bewitched" and that it is ending.

Friday:

I see pigeons flying around in circles around and around. I see people having a Birthday party and that the people are having cake and taking pictures then they dance then they see as the person opens the presents. The person is a lady. She gets towels, perfume, powder, earrings. I think it is her husband who gives her the ring because they kiss then some go little by little.

Tony Ibanez AGE 11 UNITED STATES

THREE

Animals

THE CAT AND THE DOG

Once upon a time there lived a brown cat and a black dog and one day the cat asked the dog to chase him around the kennel until he was puffed out and then their owner gave them a meat pie they loved chasing rats and mice and the cat was always stepping in the milk and making white stars on the floor so that he wouldn't get lost in the house.

Michael Delany AGE 8 ENGLAND

HOW TO TRAIN YOUR HAMSTER

When you train your hamster be very patient with your hamster and reward him when he does the trick right do not reward him if he does it wrong. Then he will see when he does the trick right you will reward him with a piece of corn or a sunflower seed then he or her will understand that when he does something right he will be rewarded with something to eat then he will always want to do a trick because he will know he will get fed and he will also learn how to trust you and you will make some friends too.

Doris Heinrich AGE 6 UNITED STATES

THE DOG WHO KISSED THE CAT

Once there was a man and a lady. They had pets. The man had a dog, and the lady had a cat. The pets were pregnant. They had their babies.

After 1 month went by the cat kissed the dog. Then the cat said will you marry me. The dog said yes. So they eloped. The cat was pregnant. She had her babies. And more and more and more babies.

Then one day one of her babies ran away and a boy saw the cat. The boy said look at that cat it is half dog. The cat said the hell you think half dragon. After that the cats were never seen.

Nathan Butler AGE 12 UNITED STATES

THE REAL CHICKENS OF THE SEA

All the fish sighed with relief; the storm was *over!* The top of the sea was calm now, but the king's anger made the bottom rumble. "Two more boats with humans in them stole 4000 more of my people!" he said. "Let the fish declare war with the humans!" As soon as the fish heard this, they swam home to hide under their seaweed beds. The king fish was screaming mad! Then he had an idea that might make the fish angry at the humans. He told the town crier to say awful things about humans. Finally the fish declared war on the humans! The king fish spent millions of seashells for the war. When the fish were ready and lined up for war, a surprising thing happened. Two boats filled up with humans took 4000 more fish. After that happened the fish swam home to hide under their seaweed beds.

Helene D. Homer AGE 11 UNITED STATES

The duck likes to blow balloons up. When he was blowing up a balloon a lion crept up and bit her up because he likes to blow up balloons. When he was blowing up a balloon a bear crept up up and bit the lion up because he likes to blow up balloons too. Then a elephant came running and gobbled the bear up and because she likes to blow up balloons too. He kept blowing up balloons and blowing them up and blowing them up and blowing them up and nobody came so he was the lucky one. Then he skipped and hopped and laughed with joy. She was so happy. She was the happy of all because all of the animals were in the tummy squeaking.

Rachel Tannenbaum AGE 7 UNITED STATES

THE FOX

One day it was a fox. He used to kill the bugs. Every day he used to get up real early. Every time something started to eat the bugs, so the bugs ran away and away.

The other bug went out in the forest. So when he was walking along he saw a snake. He went over towards the snake. The snake wiggled his tail and he bit at the bug and he swallowed that bug. So the bug went down and down. He went so far down he could not see anything. He went down in the snake's stomach.

The bug had some babies in the snake's stomach. The babies got bigger and bigger. So big that they itched the snake's stomach. He itched so bad he died. And then he dried up and you saw his bones. And the bugs got out of the snake's stomach.

So the bugs went back to the forest. Then they ran and ran till they saw the fox. The fox ran and ran to the bugs. So the fox got one of the bugs' tail. The fox cut the bug's head off. And it started to bleed. So the fox ate him. And he saw the other bug. He did the same thing. And he ate the bug raw. And that was the end of the bugs.

Alexander McNeil AGE 7 UNITED STATES

THE INSECTS' HOPE

A cockroach made his way through a bedroom into a hole where other insects were waiting. "What took you so long?" asked a bee who was the leader of the small group in the hole. "Sorry," answered the cockroach, "I was afraid." "See, see," interrupted a black ant, "all of us have to live in fear. Everybody picks on black ants, especially red ants." "Look who's complaining. Red ants are cruelly stepped on because our cousins who live far away from here have stingers!" shouted a red ant. "I say we should destroy the humans," said a flea. "Then I wouldn't live," shouted a bloodsucker, "Why don't we destroy dogs!" "First of all we don't have an army," said the bee. "We can make an army of bees and army ants," suggested a fly. "No . . . the bees will lose their stingers and die and the army ants will be killed with pesticides," said a mite. "I suppose then there is no way to live without fear," said the bee. Then the insects went home knowing there was no way, yet hoping.

Helene D. Homer AGE 11 UNITED STATES

THE HUNTER

The lady bug didn't want to see the hunter. Because he banged all the animals. The butterflies flew away, they were afraid. The bears helped the ones that were sad. They killed the hunters. The bears caught them. They got the hunters dead.

Alice Lichtenstein AGE 6 UNITED STATES

CHARLIE

Charlie is a turtle. He is just a small turtle. He crawled up on John's arm. And then he crawled back down John's arm. In John's house is where Charlie lives. He lives in a dish of water. He eats food. John always took Charlie out of his dish and put Charlie on the floor. One day when John was sleeping Charlie crawled out of his dish. And then it happened. Charlie fell out of his dish and he cracked his shell and when it was morning John saw Charlie. And that's how the story goes.

John Van Gordon AGE 7 UNITED STATES

SONG OF THE CRICKET

Nothing is better than the song the cricket sings. The sound of the cricket brightens my feelings and makes me sing too. My mind is the cricket's mind and I wish I was a cricket. Hop, hop the black cricket. The cricket pokes out his feelers and I can hold them and the song of the cricket is my mind.

Marilyn AGE 7 NEW ZEALAND

MY GOAT TINKER BELL

She lies on the hay and I lie on her. The rain drips off the roof while the rain pours outside she's warm and I like just lying there talking to her softly. It's only a small shed about four feet high and we're both squashed together but it's nice just how I like it to feel.

Susan Streeter AGE 12 NEW ZEALAND

A CAT CALLED BLACKIE

It was my brother's birthday party. He was twelve. I was only nine. He invited a lot of boys whom I did not know.

We were in the middle of a game when someone shouted out: "He's a bit young, isn't he?"

I looked towards where he was pointing; then I gasped in horror: he was pointing at me!

"Yes," shouted another, "let's get rid of him." He gave me a sharp poke in the side; my brother tried to stop him, but to no avail. Before anyone could do a thing to stop him, he had thrown me into the hall.

I walked past the sitting room into the dining room. Blackie was on the most comfortable chair as usual. I looked at him. I fell into tears. I walked forward cautiously, so as not to wake him; but he lifted up his head as if he sensed me; then dropped it again and purred. I fell beside him. As I put my head against his, I could not stop the attack of sobs that followed.

I stroked his head. He purred again. I tried to wipe the tears out of my eyes; but I could not.

I rested my head against his black furry stomach. He twitched his ears. The steady thump of his tail calmed me.

I looked at the wet on his side. The steady rhythm of his heartbeat ticked in my ears. But suddenly I could not look at him, as I remembered those boys, and how they would laugh if they saw me and my cat.

Richard Iron AGE 11 ENGLAND

TEARS IN HER EYES

Pandora is a German Shepherd dog. She loves me. She used to live with another girl but we bought her. Pandora jumps all over me and kisses me and she looks like she has tears in her eyes when she looks at me. She thinks I'm the other girl.

Laura Cominetti AGE 6 UNITED STATES

ROGER

Roger was Grandpa's cat. He lived in the flowers by the back doorstep mostly, and you'd see him looking out at you from his forest of stalks as you went to the garage or the back garden. Mum made me a mask of black cardboard that summer and I spent hours galloping up and down the lawn with the washing-line in it, and the field with the big tall trees at the end, and I wondered who lived next door, because there was always smoke coming from the chimney, because that was the highest I could see over the hedge, and I'd come back all tired out after watering Grandpa's runner beans, and I'd ask if I'd done long enough, and the answer was always no except before meals, and I'd come out, avoiding the milk-box by the metal food-scraper carefully, and there'd be old Roger, just a mass of orange fur all puffed out, hiding in the big flowers, looking at me through the tangle of green stalks.

Roger was an orange legend to me then, I was that small. When he came out from the flowers you never saw him till he showed up by the long swing-chair with creaky springs when we were all sitting on the cushion enjoying the sun and swinging and swinging, and old Roger came crawling out of the weeds and walked up to the stone bird-bath with stone rabbits all covered with green moss that was wet and cold even in summer at the bottom, and Grandma said, Look, she said, there's old Roger, and we all said yes, and I thought how he'd come through the dank, cold wood-pile at the side that had spiders as big as my hand on the walls and among the logs, because I didn't like it there; it was so dark and mossy and chilly, and I didn't like that; so I stayed on the lawn or in the sun, and we just stayed rocking in the sun and Roger blinked at the sun, and crawled off.

Grandma's dead now. We stayed at a big hotel in Southampton, and we saw Mum off in Aunt Iris's car for the funeral, because we couldn't go, and Uncle Arthur was all lurching round the place and couldn't get into the car properly so Aunt Iris yelled at him a bit and then they went off and we went indoors again, and well, it just wasn't like a funeral, somehow, and I'd never seen a grave with someone I knew in it and it wasn't all solemn and Mum got in a temper at the station because we'd caught the wrong bus and everything was all wrong, and it still wasn't like a funeral.

Roger died, too. I didn't know till Mum and Kathie said he'd been put to sleep, and how sad it all was, and it just wasn't sad, I was that young, but we're never going to rock in the sunshine again with old Roger blinking in the brightness and we're never going to ride in Grandpa's old car again, the car with the seats that smelled nice and with the brown blanket specially for Grandma but we used it too, and I'm never going to play around in my mask and see old Roger in his forest of stems, and that's sad.

Richard R. Crook AGE 12 ENGLAND

FOUR

Fantasies

THE DRAGON THAT COULD NOT BREATHE FIRE

Once in a place far, far away in the lush green fields of Laggin Lo Lake an old dragon, battered from many fatal battles, laid an egg and died.

Day by day the sun beat down upon the egg. Finally life stirred within the thick shell of the egg and a crack appeared on the surface. That day a skinny little dragon forced his way into the sunlight. Gorking and honking, as a dragon will, he clambered down the the slickery slockery sides of Laggin Lo Lake. After finishing some flickery frogs he gave a loud "gonk," but something was wrong.

Then he became worried. He was a dragon, he was sure of that, but he didn't breathe fire! What could he do? A caterpillar seeing he was in trouble asked, "Could the Cackly maid in the village help you?" So off the dragon set at a fair trot to the crumbling cottage of the Cackly maid. She placed her foot upon her head (for that's how Cacklies think, you know) and started to think thoughts. She took a lighter and lit the fire-flack at the end of his long throat.

This would be awful if it happened to you since you aren't a dragon, but to a dragon, this is very important. This is just what he needed. To this day at the edge of the slickery slockery banks of Laggin Lo Lake that dragon will be gorking and gonking—and breathing fire!

Jackie Weller AGE 10 CANADA

INVADED BY MARS

I was in my schoolroom one day when I heard a strange noise, but I thought it was the squeaky fan. When recess came I asked Raymond, the janitor's son, if the fan was squeaking, but he said his father just oiled it. Later on in the day I saw five specks in the sky, as the specks grew larger the noise grew louder and penetrated farther. Finally there was a screaming, a wailing and a buzzing noise. Great huge space ships in many colors hovered above the ground ready to land. After they landed six robots appeared from pitch black doors which automatically slid open. As they scattered the freaksom chief came out, red-eyed, steel-plated, on rollers came speedily rolling towards the school. Its hoselike arms fluttered in the spring breeze. After it had rapidly rammed through the desk and sink, it rocketed through the ceiling. Meanwhile Mrs. Indergard rang the emergency fire, everyone rushed outside. Finally Mrs. Indergard escaped the vision of the guard robot and got into the school only to find phone wrenched off of the wall and stamped into sand-small pieces. Jack and I said we could help. Soon we came back from a nearby store with a gallon jug of gas, I put a fuse into the jug and lit it with some of Mrs. Indergard's matches. Rapidly I ran into the principal's office, set the jug down and ran for dear life, but half way down the hall my runner screeched to a stop to avoid ramming a band of six robots at either end of the hallway, rolling at full speed. I screeched into my room where a table stood, after smashing a window I jumped out. I happened to look at my watch, in a second's time I knew I had 1 minute and 10 seconds. In a flash I was at the store with many other people. 1 or 2 seconds later flames, robots and smoke shot forth from the school, with a thundering roar the school exploded. At first I didn't know that another robot was still alive, after I found out that there was one, I borrowed a glass full of gas, made a fuse and set it inside the doorway. Again the explosion shot flames, smoke, space ships and a thundering roar over the fields. Since then we haven't been invaded by Mars.

Glenn Piwowar AGE 8 CANADA

THE DAY FUNGUS TOOK OVER THE WORLD

One day some doctors were operating on a very sick person.

When they got to the heart they found it was covered with fungus. They knew the person was dead but for some reason they didn't put the heart back into the patient, instead they just threw it out the window.

A dog picked up the heart in his teeth and brought it into the woods. The next day the dog just turned into a bunch of moss.

One day a man was walking through the woods barefoot when he stepped on some glass. It didn't hurt too much so he kept right on walking. He then stepped onto the heart which was now a beating patch of fungus.

When he got home he looked at his foot and there growing right out of his cut was moss. Soon he was walking through the street as a living man made of fungus.

Everything he touched turned to fungus or started growing fungus, green fungus. Instead of eyes there was fungus. The cities and towns just turned into the green moss.

Vines dangled from everything, and soon the atmosphere became fungus.

The reaches of black outer space became green.

But there was one planet that didn't get touched by this

fungus. The planet was Sanguinus. It's a small planet about three trillion miles from Pluto going southeast. It's smaller than the moon.

The people there have a fine art: making fungus.

Roger Parsons AGE 11 UNITED STATES

THE DRAGON NAMED DRAGON

One day in a place called Kabubu there was a boy who had a dragon. The boy was named Boy, just Boy; the dragon was named Dragon; so they made a good couple. Dragon was only one month old and he was class I. A good bargain—for three dimes.

Well, of course, it was long, long, too long ago he lived. This dragon named Dragon was green and blue, with a red and yellow neck. You see he had a big neck.

Well, on with my story. Boy lived in the grass with Dragon because Dragon did not like the couch. Dragon weighed 200,000,000 pounds and liked to sleep on Boy. But Boy did not like it. Boy had Anacin for stomach aches.

Steve Herzog AGE 12 UNITED STATES

PLANET ZURANGOSHRORAPLORPINGO

On the planet Zurangoshroraplorpingo the Vangolorp people live. Their king is Whatchaworpel Fizo and their queen is Watchdoinqueen. The continents are known as Vipelap, Zemsockorarulapthemoragatorels hrorpelarp, Zenper, Femperthenka, Urplankchrarp, and Feeblveetzerzetzer. It is located in the galaxy Abarapelorpagock. It has 15 moons which are called: Zempranko, Zemlaro, Zemenko, Zemfelo, Zemverko, Zemlarko, Zemurpo, Zemlemo, Zemurko, Zemlarano, Zemklunko, Zemhicko, Zem, ZemZem and ZemZemZem. Its major sport is Curango which is played with 7 men on each side and the idea is to get the Funkee-ball into the other side's zurpolurp. The language of the people is Zerploraple Archany Shrorp Zemperhiccup Vangolorp (which means the language of the Vangolorp).

THE VANCKEE TABLE OF MEASURE

linear	*weight*
15 Zemklurks = 1 Furshlinger	15 Finkledos = 1 Finedoes
5 Furshlingers = 1 Femplurger	50 Finedoes = 1 Furpel
10 Femplurgers = 1 Urp	10 Furpels = 1 Furpelel
100 Urps = 1 Urpeler	1,000 Furpelels = 1 Supedelang
10 Urpelers = 1 Urpelerer	
100 Urpelerers = 1 Zururl	

Its major form of entertainment is the Velfor Verkeeee which is almost like a movie except it has live Vangolorp on it. Its atmosphere is made up of Oxylenk, Helpufemp, Hydroshrorp, Neorklem, Carelork Dioblanko, Dio Ozonurklame and Nitrogyreonvai. Its main vegetation is the glorkface plant which covers ⅔ of the planet. Its oceans are called Zenk, Lorp, Furp and Whatsawhosa; these oceans are usually 7000 Urpelers deep and 7010 Urps long. The main form of transportation is the Cusainaplanoat which is very much like the bus except it is a Femplurger long. The money on the planet is in the shape of a dodecahodron.

MONETARY SYSTEM

10 Furpst = 1 Lingorungo
100 Lingorungos = 1 Orgnurognil
10 Ognurognils = 1 Furshlurpo
50 Furshlorpo = 1 Opralhsrurls
50 Oprulhsruts = 1 Dingle
70 Dingles = 1 Zingle
10,000 Zingles = 1 Urple
12 Urples = 1 Lurple

The people are usually 6 feet tall and some grow to 18 feet tall or 1 inch tall. They usually live to be 100 years old. The Gurks get married to the Shrorpslenk at the age of 52.

THE END

P.S. I visited them a few days ago.

Michael Olenick AGE 10 UNITED STATES

The football players run faster and faster when suddenly whirling colors appear on the field. The football players are dancing now. They begin running again but they are running in slow motion. The football is thrown and in mid air it turns into a whirling colorful grapefruit. Suddenly a siren-like sound comes from the spinning grapefruit. The pitch of the sound gets higher and it becomes piercing. It still gets higher until it is a deafening, screeching shrill. Then it stops! The grapefruit hits the ground but does not bounce up from the ground the slightest amount. But there are no football players rushing for this still grapefruit. The field is lone and empty. The only thing on the field is this one grapefruit. It begins shrinking and getting smaller and smaller. If one listens carefully one can hear a faint song which has no source.

John Auerbach AGE 13 UNITED STATES

When I was going in a big plane it was very dull. Suddenly the plane went out of order. We were heading for the ground the pilot could not see where he was going. Smash the plane crashed we were lost in the fog we were lost on an island. We didn't know what to do. But there were natives on the island they told us what to do about the fog it was the evil spirits they shifted the evil spirits for us. We repaired the plane.

Peter Cummings AGE 6 AUSTRALIA

Once upon a time there was a Greyhound bus and the people got in. One was a famous arch man and one was a government and one was a pastry man and one was a wire-fixing man and the last one was a tailor, and a man with a big beard and a moustache and lots of hair had told them that they were going to a candy store, so they got in the bus which drove and drove until it came to a gate and the man with the beard opened it and they fell down into a hole past lots of seahorse blood and turtle blood down to a place where there was a big wall with the word TRAP on it, and they noticed that in the letter "R" in the word electricity was shooting out and it was an electric wall that moved and it had sharp teeth on it, and the government said, "Hey, we're not supposed to be in here," and the tailor said, "Why this is not the right place they said. Maybe they're playing jokes on us."

The old lady who was already in there said, "I've been in here for nearly fifteen years."

And they saw that the wall with the teeth was beginning to move toward them, and just as it began to poke them, they heard a great noise BOOM that's what it was, and immediately the teeth began to fall off the wall, and then there was another BOOM and they noticed that the electric wall which had the word TRAP on it broke down. It was the old lady's husband who had a bomb, and the pirates were mad but they couldn't do anything else because it was the only one they had. They were so mad they jumped and they bumped and they pounced and then they died. Because the old wall had been broken down they climbed out and went home and they said, "I'm GLAD we're free."

Christopher Pirtle AGE 6 UNITED STATES

Professor Peaberry went to an enchanted castle. A stair broke, and he fell into a dark room. The only object was a glowing vase of white glowing flowers. He recognized it as a rare old Chinese vase with very few specimens known. A voice that sounded dead spoke.

While you are alive, forces of invisibility will trail you from this castle and watch every word you say. When you die you will awaken within the rooms of the castle. He left. . . .

Anonymous AGE 10 UNITED STATES

WHOSE HAND?

I saw a hand behind a tree and it was green. I didn't stop to see whose hand it was. I thought it was a big green man hand. And I ran and ran and ran till I was out of air. My mother and father thought I was nuts and my sisters thought I was nuts but I was not nuts.

Fred Laylin AGE 9 UNITED STATES

IT

It was a shadowy figure. It had no feelings. It was nothing. Most people called It a ghost or a spirit.

It had died one year ago in the living room of its house. It had been murdered.

It was now trying to find its murderer. It saw a figure, a man's figure. It jumped on the figure. Then It said something strange to make it appear as a human. It took a knife from its pocket and stabbed the man. It then turned back into It.

It would kill anything. Someday It would kill the murderer. It thought back to when It was human. It couldn't remember who or what it was then. It suddenly remembered. It had been eleven years old. It had been an unpopular girl with no friends. It got sad as It recalled. Then It got a feeling. It hadn't had feelings before. It started to cry. It wilted away crying and crying. It would never appear again.

Virginia Staples AGE 10 UNITED STATES

I am a ghost in a lost world. The people are strange creatures. They do not smile. They never go out of this strange world. Sometimes they look as though they are happy but I never know. The place they live in is just like a blank space on a piece of paper.

Sandra Davis AGE 9 UNITED STATES

THE ADVENTURES OF A TOY

Plenty of years ago in a cozy cottage I was I, living at the age of five. There was a terrible storm the wind howled and the snow fell and I was carried away by the wind. I couldn't stand it. So what was this? I found myself in a little house. Right in a pot of butter. I knew something was going to happen to me. Before I could even think I was a teddy bear. The little girl picked me up and was going to cook me. The Police came. But I told them not to worry. I had a time.

David Solomon AGE 6 AUSTRALIA

THOUGHTS ON BEING A HOT-WATER BOTTLE

I often wonder how it must feel to be a hot-water bottle to be filled with hot water, and to be put in a bed to go cold so very, very, slowly; then in the morning to be taken from the bed and emptied and sometimes squeezed in the process and then to be hung up only to be taken again the next night, to be filled up, to have the air pushed out and have the top screwed tightly on. I wonder if that hurts.

I am sure it must hurt at least a little bit. Then again you are put in a bed to go cold slowly. This must happen many times, especially in the winter, the coldest season of the year. Then summer comes. I wonder what it feels like to be put away in a cupboard for two seasons and have it happen all over again and again so many times. I just wonder how it feels to be filled and emptied to be hot and go slowly cold so many times.

Julie Cooper AGE 8 NEW ZEALAND

THE CUP OF TEA

The white grains fall down into the depths of the sea. A silvery enemy dives down crushing the white innocents, turning them over and into a whirlpool.

Christine Short AGE 11 NEW ZEALAND

IF I WERE AN ALKA-SELTZER

If I were an Alka-Seltzer I would be stored in a jar for days and weeks. Then people would store me in their medicine cabinet with the aspirins and the iodine. It would be boring. Then when they get ready to take me I would have to penetrate all that *bad!! breath!!* I would hold my fizz. Then after I dissolve and fizz in the stomach, I would be in a jungle of ugly stomach tubes and intestines. Then I would dissolve into that acid and drop into that drip dry part of the stomach and dissolve into nothing. And stop people's stomachs from talking.

Anthony Coleman AGE 11 UNITED STATES

CHEWING GUM

I open the packet and slowly I push out. Into the torturer's mouth it goes, trying to scream its way out, but the knives of my gum close down on it, and it struggles no more.

Graeme S. AGE 10 NEW ZEALAND

THE INCINERATOR

As I am filled up with food I get very exhausted. I become dizzy as the golden flame flows out of my mouth. I flop down and my food smolders. (Then the thing that always happens.) The small flames scream at me to let them get out. I collapse and my heart breaks into smoldering pieces as the flames get taller and tear me open.

Christine Short AGE 11 NEW ZEALAND

THE TYPEWRITER

Every now and then somebody sticks a piece of paper in Me. I don't get one thing that is I don't see why they keep on clicking Me and turning My noise and changing My best color. Every time they are done with Me they would always take the paper out of Me. And there is one thing wrong with Me that I do not get. I keep on hitting Me.

Michael Goodman AGE 9 UNITED STATES

CHESS KING'S DIARY: OCT. 27, 1952

I am tired as I look on my checkered battlefield. My Right Rook has come to me with news. He says that this bloody war is being fought by Gods who called this war a game—a game which Gods call chess. I was about to banish him for this but instead black bishop roared in and took his life away. Then I saw a big thing that looked like a crane with little spears and at the end I saw some blades—five of them to be exact. And they picked up Rook and took him away.

But what was that! Bishop and my two gallant knights have surrounded the enemy King. Slowly and softly a voice in the sky says: "Checkmate." The war is won on the field and the victory is ours. The day is glorious.

But what is this—we are being swept into . . . what! It's a monstrous box! Us and the enemy alike! It is not fair—we deserve to live. We should stay—it is not fair!!

Danny Freedman AGE 10 UNITED STATES

Once there was a man who had some gold. Whatever he said the gold would do. If he said "tree" a bit of the gold would turn into a tree, and if he said "Ham" a bit of the gold was it. Once the man said "World" and on his birthday he got a little picture of the world, and on Christmas, each birthday and each Christmas, he'd have a little picture of the world. One day on his birthday he got a silver suit: a silver pants and a golden shirt, and once he said to the shirt, "Pumpkin," but nothing happened, and he thought only the gold he had would do it, so he asked the gold for a pumpkin but nothing happened. But one day there came to the door a green pumpkin with a triangular nose and round eyes and a dreary halfway smile. . . .

Christopher Pirtle AGE 5 UNITED STATES

THE MAGIC WORD

My friend Tommy is interested in magic words. I told him that most magic words were backwards words. So Tommy said "Office" backwards and then it made me see things like white lightning that struck everything that was green and my wallpaper and blanket are green. I saw red snakes and blue snakes. And space ships and people pushing me. So I didn't get to sleep last night at all and I was almost late for school.

Eric Johnson AGE 6 UNITED STATES

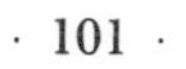

FIVE

Family Life

MY BROTHER

Once my brother wrote a story and a poem about me. I cannot write poetry so I'll write about my brother. He's very mean to me, real mean.

At 8 o'clock in the morning he opens his eyes and yells Dave. That is me and I am already for school and going to eat my breakfast. I am just putting the first spoonful of cornflakes into my mouth when I hear him yell. He thinks because he is deaf I am as well and my spoonful of milky flakes fly all over the table. Dave, means, "Bring me a cup of tea." I used to walk all the way into the bedroom one time and listen to him say "Bring me a cup of tea" but now I save time by taking it in before he asks. All the time I am pouring the tea he is shouting Dave. He should know by now that I know what he wants. I take him the tea and he wants toast. It is best not to argue because when mom isn't in I come off worst.

I eat my cold cornflakes while he lies in bed with his tea and toast. At half past eight he is out washing and I polish his shoes and find his handkerchief because although he has a chest of draws and a cabinet and a cupboard he never knows where he puts things. He drops everything he takes off on the floor and he's untidy as well as mean. My mother is going to commit suicide.

Of course his shoes are never polished to suit him. I am pleased when he goes to work and I can get warm before going to school. As if it's not bad enough having a mean brother I have to go to school as well.

Well when he comes home my brother takes the best chair nearest the fire. He takes size 11 shoes and I can't even see the fire once he's spread out and there's no chance of seeing my programmes on T.V. because he wants to watch the other side and because he is so mean I watch the other side as well.

That is when I'm not passing him the ash tray because mom goes off her head if he drops ash all over or putting the kettle on for his night shave or finding his clean underwear or picking up all the things he's dropped or going to get him cigarettes because he's walked right past the shop on his way home.

Another thing every day he promises me threepence to clean his shoes but come pay day he forgets or plays me rummy and wins it all back. I'm glad when he goes to the club and I can watch T.V. but then what happens. It's bed time.

I expect I would get hung if I murdered him but I expect he will be better when he gets over being seventeen and left school. He thinks it's made him boss because he's left school.

My mom has read this and said I'll have to see a psychiatrist and I cannot send this to you if I don't cross out the bit about her committing suicide but It's my story so I'll leave it in.

David Deakon AGE 11 ENGLAND

THE FIGHT

A thud, a yell, silence. Another thud, this time louder, a yell. Again two thuds in quick succession a terrific scream, a bounce, a crack of springs another yell. A flurry of venomous thoughts across my brain. Torture? The rack, wrist crush, under the fingernails?

Wait! A sound. Ronnie quit hitting me!!! Another squeak of springs, a crash, a crash against the wall, a violent opening and closing of doors, silence. Ten seconds later, a muffled but distinct yell, "Ronnie, let me out of the closet. Please! With sugar on top!" Silence. "Help somebody!"

Having heard heavy steps, I became very quiet. My Father! He yelled at them and told them what a good boy he was when he was a kid, then he bombed them. Chuckle, laugh. Then he left. A thud, a yell, silence!

Richard Natisin AGE 13 UNITED STATES

HURT PLACES

I've heard my mother tell people that when I was two or thereabouts, I picked up a potato beginning to spoil from the kitchen bin and said thoughtfully and with tender concern, " 'tato has a hurt place." I guess we all have our hurt places. I used to get them a lot on my knees. I'm actually proud of the ones I get in football practice. And now I'm thirteen I seem to get them more on my heart. Sometimes I feel that the Negro in our society is just one big hurt place from having been buffeted about and bruised for 300 years. I am often sorry for my poor dad when mother gets angry at him for some awkward unawareness and shouts, "You're the most untuned-in person I've ever known." This speaks of two hurt places, his and hers. It seems to me that men are just not, by nature, as tuned-in as women, or it may be that it's mothers I mean. What I am sure of is that it's what we all need to be, more tuned in, tuned in to the needs and feelings of other people, and other peoples, with less *volume* of concern on our own hurt places.

Douglas Neil Rader AGE 13 UNITED STATES

ADVICE TO A NEW-BORN BABY BROTHER

Listen brother! Because I've got some advice to give you about life and the world. The reason I'm telling you this is I've been here longer and I know the tricks of the world. People will treat you rough. They will even hurt you into knots. Never think words can't kill you because they can. They won't hurt your flesh, but they can kill the spirit. The only way to keep your spirit alive is to keep your head high and not let words get you down. Words can't kill you if you don't let them.

John Dobbs AGE 11 UNITED STATES

One day when I came home I started to act daft with the dog. We played in the room and Tinker my pet dog jumped up at me and shoved me towards the sideboard and when I hit the sideboard my head hit the vase the best vase and it fell on my head and it fell off my head and it smashed on the floor. Well there was me sitting in the middle of bits and pieces with a large bump on my head I didn't know what to do so I got some glue and started to put it back to pieces again and the vase had cracks in it and I thought if I should ever be found out and then in came my mummy and daddy I heard mummy say I think I shall go and look at my best vase, then I rushed upstairs and hid under the bed and when she saw it she played hell and I felt like a roast egg and I was full of pity I was that.

Anonymous AGE 6 ENGLAND

Dad has arrived home. His face looks furious. He paces towards the house getting faster and faster and closer and closer. His fists are waving. His face is red. Suddenly he cools down and sits with despair as his voice becomes a mutter.

Anonymous AGE 11 NEW ZEALAND

One day we were walking in the jungle. I was walking by a alligator and I didn't know I was walking by a alligator and I stepped on it by accident and it growled at me and I screamed and jumped off of it and ran home and so did my mother but my father didn't run because he was brave but he did do one thing for me. He killed the alligator for me and I was glad he killed the alligator for me. And as soon as he got home I kissed him and gave him a great big hug and I said I loved him even if I get mad at you and I say I don't love you, but no I love you all the time. "You always knew I really did love you, daddy." "Huh, well, yes I always did know you loved me LeAnn. Remember once you said even when you get mad you still love me." "Yes, oh well, I just remembered," said LeAnn to her daddy, "what I said that you wouldn't forget and remember." "Well, I did forget," said LeAnn to her daddy, and they were mad at LeAnn and LeAnn was mad at her daddy forever and never made up again.

Sherry Gower AGE 7 UNITED STATES

THE SCARY DOLL

Once upon a time there was a little girl who loved dolls. One day her birthday came up. Her mother got her a talking doll. She loved it very much. But her father hated it. One day after everybody was in bed, the doll came in to kiss her father goodnight. The father didn't know she was coming in to kiss him. When she just about kissed him he woke up. He got so scared that he took that doll and threw that doll right down the steps. Well all of the sudden the doll started to walk up the steps. Her father ran up the rest of the stairs and went in the bed and covered up. The doll went to bed with her owner. The next day she was up cooking the morning meal. But what she did to the girl's father she won't tell. So when the father ate his morning meal he died. But he only died because of his meanness.

Robin Shackelford AGE 9 UNITED STATES

MY HOUSE ON 18TH STREET

In my building at night while I'm asleep, Tony and them are bumping and making noise. Part of our ceiling fell. Some of it fell on my sister Theresa.

The children in my building like to keep a lot of noise. In the daytime they like to run up and down the halls and break lights. They crack the door and windows. And at night when we look at TV my father doesn't like to be disturbed and he says, "Stop that noise up there." But they don't hear. Sometimes he feels like jumping up through the ceiling to make them stop. When my father turns into a fire breathing dragon, my mother has to put the fire out. And then his face will turn black. And then my sisters and I be so glad that we say "yeah." Then my father puts us to bed.

Carolyn Patterson AGE 9 UNITED STATES

NOISE

I think noise is wonderful, it always means something exciting. I am the only member of the family who likes noise, and who makes it. Ever since I was a child I have loved noise.

The woman next door hates silence and when everything is silent she screams. So often late at night while in bed, I hear frequent screams, and to let her know that she is not alone, I also scream. I think this must comfort her for she soon stops after this. It certainly does not please my mother, who, too, is screaming in the end.

My friend is a door bell lover, so when she comes to call for me she presses the bell in, and leaves it ringing until the door is opened. My mother objects strongly to this, as when it is pushed out, it does not usually come out, so when I know my friend is coming I have to eat my tea by the door, ready to open it when she comes. As my mother is not keen on noise she says that my friend and I are turning her hair gray.

My father claims he is the quiet type, so he is when my mother's friend comes to tea. But when a football match is on the television, my father invites all his friends round to watch. This not only annoys my mother but me also, for, throughout the whole program (it's just as if they are at the football ground) come cheers and boos, and other remarks to encourage the teams.

My dog enjoys noise, at least he behaves as if he does, for directly anyone opens the door or knocks, he barks.

I think my dog is very clever, and I'm teaching him to

sing. I just play my mouth organ, and he begins to howl. My mother thinks he does it because he does not like the noise, but I know, and I am sure he does too, that he sings because he loves noise, just as I do.

Elizabeth Mary Watson AGE 13 ENGLAND

Once there lived a six-year-old boy. His father died before he was eight, and his mother died before he was nine. He walked down the road very, very sad and could not find food to eat. Then he found an igloo and he went inside—at least he tried to—he bumped his head. It was warm inside so he slept in it. When it was morning he thought about food for a moment. He cried and cried until his face turned red. He was very sad. He fell in the cold snow and began crying again. Then an old man came and said, "What is the matter?" The boy looked up and said, "Grandpa, I thought I was going to die."

Karri Lundy AGE 7 UNITED STATES

GRANDPOP PICKING FLOWERS

Grandpop bends to pick some flowers; he is like a seagull with a broken wing. When he goes to get in the car he slowly puts one foot in then the other and now he has to put his head in. I look sadly at him and as I look at him I know that he will have a tear coming down his face.

Queenie Davies AGE 10 NEW ZEALAND

MY REAL FATHER

My Father is on the broadside and tallside. My father was a hardworking man and he had a lot of energy. He was not fat or thin. His name was Frank McHugh. He was on the healthy side. His age was about thirty years when he died, he had a good reputation, he is a married man. When he was in hospital I went to see him every Sunday afternoon. I asked him how he was going on, he told me he was getting a lot better. My father was very kind to me and he gave me and my cousins cigarette cards. He likes doing woodwork my father for me and he likes a little game of cards now and then; or a game of darts. He chops the wood and saws the planks. And he is a handsome man but he is dead. He worked at the rubber works before he died.

Anonymous AGE 9 ENGLAND

My mother is a pretty lady. I wish to kiss her all day but I have to go to school.

Tanya Price AGE 6 AUSTRALIA

I remember when I got mad at my mother and went into my room to cry. It was raining outside and I saw a mystic fog. It frightened me.

Soon I got so sleepy and tired of being mad that I fell asleep. I dreamt I flew out of bed into this mystic fog. I traveled through it wondering where it would leave me. I saw people mysterious and strange. I was too scared to do anything so I fainted.

And in a few minutes I was up and out of bed and down to dinner.

Ernie Rubinstein AGE 9 **UNITED STATES**

THE VACUUM CLEANER

My mother told me to vacuum the floor. So I got out the vacuum cleaner and started to vacuum the floor. In just a few minutes the vacuum cleaner started to wiggle around! I hit it very hard with a block of wood. That made it very angry and it sucked me up.

Karen Reed AGE 9 UNITED STATES

We were going to the clothes store and by the time we got there, Melinda and Cynthia were all thirsty. And you know how Cynthia drinks: she dribbles all over my mommy's shoes and she dribbled all over her shirt, all over Cynthia's shirt. And then by the time she got to the clothes thing by the front door, and my mama was busy picking out clothes, and then the people were starting to laugh and then my mommy turned around and there was Cynthia: she had took off her shirt and then she was trying to get off her undershirt. And her belly was sticking out.

Sorena Fee AGE 5 UNITED STATES

WHEN I WAS THREE YEARS OLD

When I was three years old I used to look at my older sister a kooky way. Every time I did this she would say: Mommy she is looking at me the way she doesn't know me any more. So then Mommy would say Robin don't do that anymore. But I did it anyway and she hated it and hated it. But I hardly ever got in trouble because I was too young.

Robin Shackelford AGE 9 UNITED STATES

A GAME OF DENTISTS

The night before I went to the dentist's, my sister and I were playing at dentists. She stamped on the floor that made the chair go up. She then switched on a light. She used a pair of pliers out of my tool set for the pinchers. She used my bubble hat for the gas mask. She used a pudding dish for the thing that you spit your blood into. She used a poker for the drill and a glass of water for the mouth wash. She tied me to the chair with some thick string and tied a hanky round my neck. She got a lolly stick and pressed my tongue back to see which tooth to pull out. She put a bit of rock in my mouth to keep it open and put my bubble hat on me. She took it off and got the pair of pliers and pretended to pull out my tooth. She took a look at it and then gave me the water and I pretended to wash out my mouth. She untied the hanky but she didn't untie me from the chair. She hit me about ten times and then ran off. I shouted mum to come and untie me. After that next time we play she's definitely going to be the patient.

Simon Mark Abbey AGE 8 ENGLAND

MY HUGGING BROTHER

My brother hugs me more than anything. But sometimes he hugs mom too. And he hugs her when she's working and makes her mad. But when he hugs me I stop working. And when he hugs he hugs. He might be small but he still can hug your legs.

Christy Moffett AGE 9 UNITED STATES

Sometimes when you meet your relatives you think you're a lollipop.

Paul Uhlir AGE 13 UNITED STATES

THE GIANT

Sometimes when I play in the garden with my Brother Andrew and when I climb up the Pear tree I seem as I was a giant. I feel as I could get onto my roof and stretch my arms in the sky and get to clouds and play with them, and I could be across the road without waiting and pick up people that looked like ants, and could pull up swings, and houses, and then tell my mother.

Jeremy Roberts AGE 6 ENGLAND

SIX

Other Children

OF ALL THE STRANGE PEOPLE I HAVE MET

Of all the strange people I have met Joey is the most peculiar. Nice boy but dandruff. He is very creative which is both good and bad.

He is head of an acting group, has a very artistic mind, and is involved in anything that involves him. There being creative is good.

He also likes to pretend he is from a backwards country. He made up his own language which is queer (as Joey would say, "Spelled with a capital Q"). There creativeness is bad.

In all what I'm trying to say is, well, Joey is kind of a sonic boom with dirt on it.

David Spiro AGE 11 UNITED STATES

MY IRRITATION

My one and only irritation is Jon. All day long he uses my pencils, music, thoughts, and papers. Does he ever make me mad! According to him, you would think he owned me. Once in a while he gets all excited and says I'm doing the wrong thing when he's doing the wrong thing.

He likes to put fleas and paper in my hair. When we're singing he sings about four notes lower and sticks in a few sharps to get us off. Jon likes to pull out chairs and stamp on my feet and everything you can think of. He's really a pain in the neck. But he's still all right.

Sandie Thorkildson AGE 11 UNITED STATES

THE PUNCH FROM SAM

One day Joe Nash was walking by Sam the girl. Just then Sam punched Joe in the eye. Then he went home. Hey mom! Sam punched me in the eye. Why didn't you punch him back? I don't know. Joe come here. Okay mom. Put the spoon on your eye. Just then dad came in. What are you doing, dear? I told Joe to do it. That's an old trick grandma told me. The next day Joe was punched again. Mother said put the spoon on your eye. The next day there was a carnival. The twins went with their mother and father and Joe. Joe saw Sam there. Just then Sam kicked Joe. Dad asked why don't you kick him? It's a girl dad.

Michael Mantell AGE 7 UNITED STATES

THE PEN LOSER

There is a girl in our school and she loses a pen a day. She is always on her knees under the desks looking for it. She spends more time on the pen than she does at her lessons. Her pet sentence is I-have-lost-my-pen. She is a tiny little girl and has a very big mouth for her size. I'm sure she would burst if she had to keep a secret.

Mary Cleary AGE 12 IRELAND

A LOST TOY BOAT

Helplessly the toy boat is thrust forward with each of the sea's powerful waves. On each undertow the toy boat is pulled back vigorously. Back and forth, back and forth, helpless, being pushed to sea. The little boy who owns it is standing watching it, knowing that that is the last time he'll see the boat again, tears slowly appear in his eyes as the water goes rushing into the little boat. It breaks below the water's surface. The little boy feels coldness and hatred toward the sea. He walks away crying. When he has left, the little boat surfaced on its back and drifted out to sea.

Andy Rowland AGE 9 UNITED STATES

There was a little boy standing right beside a car; he was crying. Tears were coming out of his eyes. He looked very sad. A man came over to him and put his face on his, and the man was holding his hand and said, "What is wrong?"

But he was still crying.

Pamela Prial AGE 8 UNITED STATES

A LOST VIET NAM CHILD

As I looked upon the lost Viet Nam child, I felt sad for her. I saw a ghost fly over this child. The child was torn within with sorrow and fear. Her heart was broken. The sadness of dark space had found a home in this child.

John Dobbs AGE 11 UNITED STATES

SPYING

One day I was spying on Karen when my friend came. He is Karen's brother. We spied on her together. When she went to the swing we went to the woods, where we could see her best. She wanted to play with us so we had to run when she saw us. Later she caught up with us so we were in a jam. We had to play with her instead of spying.

James Hunter AGE 10 UNITED STATES

MY GIRLFRIEND

My friend Sue was like a friend of all times. She was nice to her mom and sisters. She was also a friendly kid to me too.

But she's moved to across the street and has gotten to be a terrible mess. She starts fights now.

But last year she was going to the store with me. And she had fifteen cents and I had sixteen cents. So she was choosing her candy and accidentally she picked up an extra piece. But she put it in her pocket to get even with me. And now she's my X girlfriend.

Christy Moffett AGE 9 UNITED STATES

It was a nice morning when I woke up and I was in a happy mood. It wasn't until I arrived at school that I found that a friend of mine happened to be in a bad mood. The others and I were very excited about what we were playing but my friend—no. She wanted to play another game and had to have it her way. I said to myself—everyone likes it her way sometimes. She went away to play another game and we carried on. We haven't been getting on too well but she is still a friend to me. We argue all the time and fight and it doesn't stop until someone gets hurt or tells. Every day I keep on hoping and thinking that we will make it up to each other and be friends as we were before.

Margaret Hall AGE 12 NEW ZEALAND

LOVE

Two friends playing together. And love is when you like to play when he wants to and you may not want to.

David Wilson AGE 7 UNITED STATES

LIFE IS LIKE

Life is like going through a girl's room; a rambling mess as far as you can see. You have to step carefully or you'll shatter emotions and faith. Two flies are in the corner fighting a senseless war over a piece of bread. In a heap are discarded toys and remembrances.

Live well now, for in the end we all must lose. The room must get cleaned and sorted. We must die and the dog will get the bread.

Lauren Faure AGE 12 UNITED STATES

GIRLS

If there weren't any girls there would only be one generation, and after awhile they would die. And there wouldn't be any life on earth. But keep your fingers crossed.

Merrill Mason AGE 7 UNITED STATES

Girls are a lot of fun because they are feminine and nice. I should know. Some kids my age hate them, but I don't. They think girls are sissies, but they're not. They're just tender. Like Debbie. That's about it.

Roy Mitchell AGE 9 UNITED STATES

RICHIE'S FRIEND

Once upon a time there was this girl named Valerie More. And Richie liked her Richie kissed her and they did the tighten-up and then they did the cha-cha and the four corners and she didn't know his name was Dicky. Then once upon a time she knew his name was Dicky and she said Hey Dicky Dicky.

Ianta Washington AGE 9 UNITED STATES

MY FRIEND

My boyfriend's name is Bobby. He told James to ask me to go with him. And then I said I don't know. And then Bobby said that you have to give an answer. And I said okay.

And then one day when I was going home I was waiting downstairs for my brother and Bobby gave me a wink and I saw him.

Ianta Washington AGE 9 UNITED STATES

A MISTAKE THAT COST A BOY'S FEELINGS

Everything was going along fine for these two. They saw each other every day. The boy liked the girl, and he thought she liked him. He used to look at her in such a way that said he liked. They were so young, and the feelings ran so deep.

This one day, as they were sitting in the cafeteria, another boy walked up and said to move over and make room for him.

So this boy sat down when room was made. This put the pair very close together. The girl got mad and pushed the other boy off the bench. Then the girl asked, "Why are you doing this?"

The boy replied jokingly, "*He*'s paying me five cents."

This ruined everything. The boy's feelings were shattered, and the girl walked away.

The boy moped and moped. He couldn't think of what to do. She kept her distance.

Things still stand this way between them.

John Begley AGE 13 UNITED STATES

YOU

You have such a nice look on your face when I look at it. I admire it very much. And you are very warm and nice to stay with often. I think you are the nicest person to stay with. When you are not here my brain goes off and on thinking of you. But another time I didn't because I was so busy I couldn't think about you. But when I am through with it I can. I am sure it takes a long time to do that work. Who else should I think of but you. When I've had enough of work I always take a break to think of you.

John Kyriakis AGE 7 UNITED STATES

SEVEN

Myself

I am a I am a I am a I really do not know.

Josh Neubauer AGE 10 UNITED STATES

HOW I LOOK AND HOW I FEEL

I have blue eyes and blond hair which makes me feel pretty. I have freckles on my nose and on my arms. I have one nose, two eyes, one mouth, two ears, and one head with a brain inside. All that stuff is on my head. The other stuff is down below. I have two legs and two arms which I use. The inside I have a brain like I said before. And I've a heart which I love with and a lung which I breathe with and I've bones and I have veins which carry my blood inside. Those are all the things that are inside me. But wait a minute! I feel something inside. I feel young and pretty and happy and nice to other people.

Alissa Guyer AGE 7 UNITED STATES

HOW STUPID I AM

I am so stupid I don't even know how to say my ABC's. I'm so stupid I don't even know how to say *one*. I'm so stupid and dumb I can't even talk. I'm crazy, ugly and stupid and don't know nothin. Don't even know my colors but red. I can't even read, I can't even talk, I'm so stupid and dumb. Soon I went to a psychiatrist because I was crazy. I don't even know how to hardly talk. They tried to shoot me when I was at the psychiatrist's but they missed because it wasn't nothing but a puppet of me. The puppet had feathers inside of him —that's how he was different. All of a sudden something hit me in the head. I knew how to say my ABC's, I knew how to read, I knew how to say my colors, I knew how to write, I knew how to do everything.

Enid Talbert AGE 8 UNITED STATES

FEAR

I fear either people that might kidnap me or something like that. Or that the wind will push me into the slush or I'll slide right into a car. Sometimes I think that the bus driver is under a threat and that the bus will explode.

Marina Heau AGE 10 UNITED STATES

FEAR

It is school for the third time this year. I've had my breakfast and wash and am down in the lounge behind the sofa looking for my other sock.

A cold hard cover seems to spread itself over my body, the hairs on my legs and arms stand up on end. I shiver and shudder from head to foot. A cold, hairy, tickly body walks underneath my cardigan, down my arm. I put my hand over it, it's a round thing with legs. I can't move, I try to scream, but nothing comes out. My hand lifts up the edge of my cardigan and a huge black spider runs out. I shake it off and open my mouth and scream but only a squeak comes out. I stand up and run out from behind the sofa and start crying in fear. I tremble and shake and my mind is in a blur. Angela my sister comes down the steps and asks me, "What's the matter," I feel like hitting her. She goes up and asks mum what the matter is with me. Mum's in a bad mood and so is dad. Mum asks me "What's the matter" and when I tell her she says don't be so stupid and hurry up and get those socks and shoes on. I ended up going out of the door sobbing in fright. I still haven't got over it properly and at night I feel prickly as though there are lots of spiders crawling all over me.

Susan Streeter AGE 12 NEW ZEALAND

There are two worlds one with eye balls facing out and one facing in. My eyes are in and the world I live in looks pretty good. There are long skinny red and blue tubes that's my water supply. It is always dark I'm scared.

George Semper AGE 10 UNITED STATES

It is awful. I will break. I will open and drop my troublesome passenger. None but he can hurt me. The other clouds laugh at my agony. Ha, ha, ha, they say. I burst in sorrow.

Amy Schwartz AGE 10 UNITED STATES

I'm not sad. I'm just frowning a very little bit. That's at the very back. Sad is further up, and moaning, and being dead is at the very front. I'm at the back.

Christopher Pirtle AGE 5 UNITED STATES

Here's a funny clown who's in another fire and he's all in the fire. His clothes are on the hanger in the fire. And he's kicking the fire and he's got his face in the fire. And he's licking the fire and he's screaming for help and his house where his parents in they heard him and they put their hand at the stone and they feeled and they went in the stone and they were with him. And the parents were dead.

Tammy MacGregor AGE 5 CANADA

FROM A MADMAN'S DIARY

Oct. 24, 1964.

They were tolling. . .

Those bells. . .

They remind me of claws. Why? I don't know. Today I felt happy. I killed a flower. Really and truly killed it. I don't like color, I want to squeeze, squeeze out the essence of what is colored. Why was there a God to invent color? I hate, hate him. I don't like color. I've said it!

Oct. 26, 1965.

I didn't want to write those days. I felt bad. I felt speed today. It was lovely hearing the noise of speed—Rrrrrr—ush—that's how the noise went, I want to remember it for ever the noise. Why don't people listen to me, my noise; my talk, how silly people are? Am I a person?

Jan. 28, 1966.

Why I like paper, I never knew that I did, Paper you lovely thing! But what I like I can't do anything, can I? I can adore, but I can't touch; So paper I can't write upon. A pity. I don't like paper then.

Do people outside do the same thing as me? Change opinions without reason? But no, I have a reason, a good one.

Deepa Dhanraj AGE 9 INDIA

I have a special something among my brains that protects me from sunburn. It's a kind of bone, and the power from it sneaks out a little hole and goes down to my skin and protects me from sunburn.

Christopher Pirtle AGE 4 UNITED STATES

LONG HAIR

To me long hair represents evil. It looks dead. Just picture, dangling looking as if it were on the hangman's noose. It gives me a dull gloomy feeling when I think of it. But it's mysteriously alluring. It's simply beautiful. It's just like a spider coaxing its victim into its web.

Sheryl Golob AGE 11 UNITED STATES

TRAPPED

To be what I am is not always what I relish. Why can't I change to something else whenever my life is too much to bear? Like an innocent speck of dust on a table. What freedom! To blow around on a breeze, dodging dust cloths! Aha!

Or maybe I could be a mosquito so I could bug everyone who has ever bugged me. A thought-thirsty fiend, I'd be. Ha, I'd be the brightest mosquito around, that is, until I got squashed.

Or maybe I'd portray another person, and see the world from another vantage point. Look upon myself in thought from far away. What does another person think of me? Do I dare try to find out?

Still, to be what I am is not always what I relish.

Nancy Lynn Clark AGE 11 UNITED STATES

Rush, rush, rush, rush to the moon, rush to school, rush to war, rush to stick your nose in everyone's business but your own, don't stop, if you do, the other "rats" will run you down. Of all the things mankind needs most, it's leisure. We need the ability to plop down in an overstuffed chair and relax. One way is to forget *everything,* let the others rush along their merry way. Join the few sleepy slowpokes plodding along the sidelines. Another way is to slow down. Let all the others pass you by, sooner or later, something will snap. Leaving one less in the race, who is buried in the sod the rest have kicked up. Leisure assures a longer life, yes, but most get bored with it, and head back toward the race track, to pit their speed against chance and the other racers. For what.

Barbara Huber AGE 12 UNITED STATES

MONEY

At the sight of a greenback and the tinkle of some change, I am beginning to fall into a deep love with money. Of all the money of the world (and I love all money), I am going crazy over American cash. Ah! But I love the kyat, the yen, the lira, I love them all, but none as much as that of America. Woe! and alas! but we cannot have gold! Gold, gold, gold, my heart pleads for ye, ye source of all money. Oh! but I must settle for the paper notes, the lovely paper notes, and the beautiful coinage. And behold, I am small, and given small. But I want Big, big, big, Big in Money, money, ye source of all pleasure. Money, all power derives from thee. I want to be a millionaire, a billionaire, a trillionaire. I want the mints, and Ft. Knox.

Oh! I crave for ye, money. I love you, I need you, and I want you Oh Money. O money, I do, believe me, but my mother doesn't approve.

William Alexander AGE 11 UNITED STATES

PULLING THINGS OUT OF MY POCKET AFTER HALLOWEEN

Gum, chocolate covered raisins, another gum, chicken feed. This is Elephant, the crab. Halloween candy. I have so much jujubes and candy in my house. I steal them from the kitchen. Taffy, butterscotch, chiclets, raisins, comic books, crabs. Chiclets, taffy, butterscotch, jujubes, another chiclet. A creepy, a comic, taffy again, covered raisins. A ghost, a white sheet, candy, raisins, bubble gum, jelly beans—purple, my favorite gum. A castle of candy. Creepies, an elephant. Covered candy again. Stole it from the kitchen. Chicken feed, covered raisins, jujubes.

Bellyache from too much candy. Bubblegum, jelly beans, raisins, bubblegum again, chiclets for later. Root beer, jelly beans, checkers, a bellyache, chicken feed, lollies, getting all the candy.

Alex Frome AGE 7 UNITED STATES

PEACE/WAR

Peace is like a quietness of war. It is in heaven of the quiet. Peace is like an island of nobody around and lonely. War is like an interruption of peace. Killing all over every country. Blood shed from the foot to head of wars. Allies invading, killing, and destroying.

Where I most like to live: peace and quiet like I explain. Up in St. Louis. No terrible happenings. It would be so quiet that you can hear a worm walking across a sidewalk. It is a good place to get a suntan. I would say that everybody would like to live there.

James Elio AGE 11 UNITED STATES

I'm always losing my temper. I just cannot control my temper. First one little problem then another and another and then—one day some person hurts my feelings and I bust. I blame everything on them. And I'm always getting everything wrong. I'm just terrible. I'm also a little greedy. I'm always saying I hate people. I'm not very smart. Hardly anybody likes me. Sometimes I lie. And I'm very untidy. And I'm always making people yell at me. And I have a terrible memory. Sometimes I get so angry I want to run away. I'm always making such a lot of noise so my mother can't sleep or my father in the morning. This is what goes on. Ring, the alarm clock goes off and I wake up then I yell down to my sister and say Time To Get Up. My mother wakes and tells me to be quiet and the day begins.

Anonymous AGE 9 UNITED STATES

WHAT MAKES ME ANGRY

What makes me angry is when someone annoys me to the extreme end. Another thing that makes me angry is when someone gets in trouble and blames me for it and I get in deeper trouble. Then he wants to fight and get me into more trouble. Another thing that makes me angry is lies. I hate lies. That's why I keep good company. Children who don't fight, who don't tell lies, I try to keep company with. And you should try to keep good company too.

Alfred Abraham AGE 11 UNITED STATES

When I get angry I feel so mad I feel like I am running barefoot up a rock road.

George Semper AGE 10 UNITED STATES

ANGER

It feels like all the hatred in the world has gone into you and you just have to blow up. So you just have to let it out so you scream and kick to let it out. But always there will be a little left in you.

Anonymous AGE 10 UNITED STATES

MY TEACHER'S OPINION OF ME

I do not think my teacher likes me at all. It looks as if I'm the devil and she the angel who hates me. Every time something happens my teacher always looks at me. Like when she says we can talk and then she tells us to stop and some people keep on talking my teacher always looks at me with a mad face and writes something in her book, or when I don't have my glasses on she just says get out or says that did it you're getting out of this class, then maybe a note's going home to your mother just a few times she reminds me, and, I'm sorry to say I don't think she likes me at all.

Joseph Blanco AGE 11 UNITED STATES

THE SILENCE OF GUILT

I just stood there. "What were you doing? Why did you do it? You must grow up and forget your 7-8-year-old playfulness, and think of being sensible. Anyway, why were you fooling about? It can't be all that much fun. Can't you enjoy yourself without fooling about?"

I ran my nail along the cracks in the table, not knowing what to say, and wishing I did, or had the courage to admit it.

People were running about outside and shouting. I felt very awkward, and wished I was with them. I just said, "Well . . . I'm not quite sure, sir."

"What you mean is that you'd rather not say, isn't it?"

I said, "Well . . . ," trying to make it sound outrageous, and looked down at my finger drawing patterns on the table by scratching the varnish.

I could see by looking up at him once or twice that he was looking straight at me, and, maybe, hoping I would say something. I glanced out of the window, and could still see his eyes staring straight at me.

We just stood there, I not knowing what to say; he knowing what to say but waiting.

I thought, "Well, I'm not going to say anything," and wondered what he would say. My inward appearance was very brave and cheeky; my outward appearance, just a look of guilt and uneasiness.

As soon as the bell went, I thought he would say I'd better go, but he kept on smiling, as though sarcastically, and kept on staring at me.

I sucked in my breath as though saying "Well, we haven't

got anywhere," and maybe there was a hint of "and you've been wasting my time," which I did not mean. I suppose he thought that I had been thinking that I would behave myself from then on.

"Think about it," he said.

Roland Fidao AGE 12 ENGLAND

ME

When anyone asked me to write a story or a poem or a play I always sit for such a long time thinking what to write about and in the end, if it's at school I get into trouble because I left it so long I don't write anything and if I do write I spell it all wrong and get into trouble for that, so it's just as bad any way.

I've been kept behind at school today because I do not attend to my teacher during lessons. He told me I must write two hundred lines of three words. Look Listen and Learn. It's on the blackboard so I can spell it right. Look Listen and Learn Look Listen and Learn Look Listen and Learn Look Listen and Learn. I'm fed up. Each time my teacher said Look Listen and Learn he hit me on the head with his knuckles. That is to make it sink in. If I looked and listened all day and night I would not learn because I am a dope.

I start off listening because my teacher has a loud voice and you can't help listening to it and if he thinks I'm not listening he bangs on his desk and makes me jump and I look because sometimes his false teeth drop down a bit on some words and he makes a little slurruppy sound when he catches them up with his tongue. I look for them to fall right out on to his desk and sometimes he thinks I am interested in the lesson because I look for ages to see them drop out but he always manages to catch them up in time.

He's got hairs sticking out of his ears and when he scratches his chin they waggle in and out. I am the awfulest boy in the world because I would much rather look at his teeth drop and his hairs waggle than look at the blackboard.

My teacher is like the Vicar I used to know in Kent, always on about going to heaven. I do not think I shall go to heaven because my friend isn't going. Johnny wants to see the devil and if he doesn't go to heaven I won't. Johnny is a bit more wicked than I am, sometimes I hate him and we fight but he is my best friend.

I wish there would be a power cut then I would not have to do these lines but nothing ever happens the way I want it. I have a lucky charm on a chain round my neck but it doesn't work. I always get caught out in things but Johnny never does. Once I found a shilling in the garden when we lived in Kent. I thought it was some buried treasure but I dug a big hole and did not find any more. Mom was mad about the hole, it was where she put the seeds. People get mad very easy. I expect I will have to stay in again tomorrow night because I just saw my teacher go home and I am going because there's *Just William* on the T.V. and he's my favorite.

David Deakon AGE 11 ENGLAND

I am a person that is not any other living soul or plant. I am myself.

Katharine Trowbridge AGE 10 UNITED STATES

EIGHT

Nights

It's day and the room is fresh and welcoming. The aroma of rugs and the forbidding smell of musty bookshelves up at the top shelf where my brother keeps his gadgets of all the room. The pale gold rays of sunlight on the beds, floors and walls of the room with comfortable thoughts that make beds very inviting. The cool feeling in the cupboards and where the shadows of darkness find refuge during the day. The shadows of the trees nearby the windows spread their dark dictations which dominate the table and on parts of the beds and shelves.

The day goes by rapidly. The sun goes down to rest and the rays of the sun get fainter and fainter and darker and bigger shadows come. They get darker and bigger till it's their period and time. They creep out of the cupboards after being imprisoned. No more is the room welcoming, no more is it inviting. The ticks of the old grandfather clock get louder and louder and like a deep jet black Octopus slowly spreads its jet black ink called darkness which devours all light slowly eating its way through the room till there's nothing left but it.

Timothy AGE 10 NEW ZEALAND

MAGIC

I know how daytime changes to nighttime. Daytime melts.

Josh AGE 5 UNITED STATES

MY OWN RIVER BANK

My own river is quiet and some times you can hear a bird whistling like a soft pat sound. And breezes hitting the leaves. The water rattling softly. And sometimes I sneak out at night and go to my river and smell the breezes.

Scott Welke AGE 9 UNITED STATES

Trees that hang their heads below the earth's paws. The darkness, it's dark nothing is there, there's music yes, you can hear music, now it fades just like the darkness. Now it's all dark, nothing is there, nothing at all, silence it's all dead silence. The children in the darkness of the night, playing.

Sarah Morris AGE 11 UNITED STATES

THE DARKNESS

The stillness of the darkness can be heard and seen, disturbed only by the sound of the T.V. set and of the cars coming and going. The cool crisp air flows into my body making it cold. I gaze up at the sky and see the stars flickering through the clouds and a sudden feeling that the sky never ends passes through my mind.

Ian Wilson AGE 12 UNITED STATES

I snuggled in my bed like a rose closing.

Rhonda Lynn Mabry AGE 7 UNITED STATES

QUIET

Quiet is a splendid time when the mind thinks but sometimes you think of things that make you cry. Quiet is a little boy snugged up in bed with his teddy bear but it sometimes means when you are all alone at night and sit outside looking at stars and you can hear the crickets going away singing to each other. Quiet is when you sit next to a pond listening to the fish and ducks but we all know quiet can mean death and the tears fill the ground.

John Garry AGE 11 UNITED STATES

PAUL'S GHOST

Last night I didn't have a good night's sleep. I went to bed and a ghost came in at 8 o'clock. First he went into the bathroom and brushed his teeth slow with my toothbrush. Then he pulled the covers out on the side where I usually get out and in and then he pulled the covers out on the side where I don't usually get out and where if I do I fall kaboom! That's why I fell kaboom this morning.

I saw all of the ghost. He doesn't have any legs. He's white and about as tall as me. And he didn't beat my brains out either. I was sleeping like this—snore, snore. That's why he came in. He heard me and came through the window. Good thing a skunk didn't come in.

Paul Rawlins AGE 6 UNITED STATES

BEFORE I GO TO BED

Before I go to bed I look under the bed and I look inside the closet because I think there might be a man and then I look out the backyard and look at the trees and say to myself the way the days go by and I am wasting them, soon I'll die and my children will waste them too. I go to bed then I start thinking about boys and about the future then I pray and I turn off the light and I dream all black, but sometimes I dream about all sorts of things. Once I had a dream and I woke up crying. And the other day I was dreaming that I was with my father and these two were looking for him to kill him and then I got in the way and they stabbed the knife at me. Then all of a sudden I wake up and call my brother and tell him it's time to go to school. And that is what I do before I go to bed.

Nereida Mendez AGE 14 UNITED STATES

MONSTERS

When I think of monsters I think of great, fat, hairy spine-chilling dinosaurs or dragons with flames sprouting from their crimson red jaws, with massive teeth smoldering in flame. Sometimes I think of the Loch Ness monster, wet, slimy and covered in warts. Ugh! My body would freeze at the thought of these overpowering monsters. Then I would cast my thoughts into my mind where many fictitious monsters live. They lurk where nobody can physically sense them, only by spiritual means. I then think of the nicer monsters —though none can be good—human monsters. These have been laughed at, put on show and even killed. That is the sad side of monsters.

Martin Lee AGE 11 ENGLAND

THE NIGHTMARE

Once there was a man and he was out in his ship all alone and it was night. And suddenly all the waves came bigger and he looked up at the stars and they came bigger. He felt scared. The stars came very big and then they burst into big snowflakes. The snowflakes began to open very slowly and out of the snowflakes came witches and ghosts and all sorts of scaring things. Then all the snowflakes turned very little, and then they changed back into stars and the stars went little. The witches' ghosts and all the other things came down to the man and began to shake him. It was really a nightmare and just then he woke up and his wife said, "Take this drink of orange and have a game of cards with me and it all will pass out of your mind." And all the time it was night.

Jacqueline Lesly Wright AGE 7 ENGLAND

SINGING STARS

They shine and tingle in the night. And in the dark they move around and all at once they tingle together as always.

Patty MacNeil AGE 8 UNITED STATES

When all is silent, nothing moving, nobody talking, you have a very lonely feeling confronting you. You feel as if nothing exists to make such a noise. All is still. It is almost like death to break the stillness and silence. When you are watching a piece of dust moving, and nobody else is there, then you hear the silence, you can feel the quiet about you. It feels like a very soft humming noise of voices from nowhere, when taking a rest and there is still only you. It feels very different, you just have to move to break that silence. Also when all is silent and you hear someone speaking very softly then it feels quiet, as if the world has stopped turning.

Anonymous AGE 10 NEW ZEALAND

NINE

Endings

Shh—silence, splash the sound of seagulls the silence of nowhere is there while the sea rocks itself to sleep.

Gina Roose AGE 9 UNITED STATES

THE WAVE

As I stood alone in the dark blue sea, a wave sprang up from behind me, my heart missed a beat as I shielded my eyes. My ears were throbbing and my hands were shaking, it seemed to be waiting for me to run. But I stood there rooted to the ground, then suddenly I sank down with it.

Michael Freeman AGE 11 ENGLAND

SEAWEED

The devil's discarded cloak on the sand's damp hard surface,
taunted by the sun which dries it out of existence.

Carin LaGro AGE 13 NEW ZEALAND

It looks very bad to be an old tree trunk. You are all broke up. And little animals coming into me making homes.

Arlanda McCoy AGE 10 UNITED STATES

To touch an old person's hand is to touch the scales on a dry fish. To be a giant touching frozen river veins.

David Urrows AGE 10 UNITED STATES

SILENCE

The steps creak as the old man walks down them. The banister cries as his dingy hands slide on them. The air suffocates as the man takes up its absence.

Michael Goodman AGE 10 UNITED STATES

DYING

It feels to have had a good day that came to a stop. To feel like a person in a maze, the maze of life, and come to a dead stop. The stop of life.

David Urrows AGE 10 UNITED STATES

Falling dying twinkling with hope but crying expecting something sort of sadness not found anywhere in the velvety never ending universe of dying things . . .

Sara Maltz AGE 10 UNITED STATES

THE GRAVES

They are still. All over.

Ngaire AGE 9 NEW ZEALAND

WIND

The wind from above, came down, down, down to freeze us all. Cold wind, fierce wind, dry wind.

Beating on our faces till dusk.

Pine trees bow to the wind.

But the grass just laughs in vain. The wind is cold, the wind is dry. The wind is fierce, strong and fierce and it runs through the wood, blindly, madly running. The wind is the fallen chestnut tree. Branches, leaves whipped about, lying down dead. The wind is broken slates on the path, birds' nests on the ground, eggs smashed, yolk about.

John Downey AGE 10 IRELAND

I left through the portal. Below, above, around I could see the grand vista of this world. The desert stretched out, the rocky crags the only markers of reality. I knew that they, although seeming minute, were huge on the normal scale of things. The sun was setting. As its last rays glanced over the horizon I lifted my head and looked up. The image of the star-clothed sky seemed fantastically real. I looked below and saw that I was rising swiftly upward. The earth was shrinking behind me. The beauty of the scene was blinding. Speeding through clusters of stars, seeing the universe shrink behind me, the blackness seemed to close in. There were no more stars, no landmarks, no movement. Time and space did not exist. I walked to the edge of the black chamber and opened the door I knew to be waiting. As I left life, I knew my body to be the food for passing creatures in the desert behind me.

Pepi Karmel AGE 12 UNITED STATES

BLINDNESS

It is a black jar or a dark tunnel with no opening to the world outside. The fog drifts around me. I try to break it. But it lasts forever and ever.

There are no lights. It knows no shadows. There is only the deep, rich black. Tear a hole in it to reach day. There is no day, but everlasting night so dark. Does day ever break?

The soul beneath sees a different dazzle. The mind reaches far and forever not like the breath that dies and never comes again.

Lori Schectman AGE 10 UNITED STATES

HELL DEEP

Not black. Black is mercy. Just gray. But not clear. Misty. Thick. No sight—nothing to see. Nothing to hear.

Sweet, heavy hanging smell, that poked and choked—and dulled. No thinking. Nothing to think. Not warm—not cool, no temperature.

Walk, walk, onward into nothingness. Walk on forever. Walk in death.

Thomas Fosha AGE 14 UNITED STATES

A person walking in black boots walks to the gloomy and foggy world and disappears in the mist and just floats away where nobody can see him. Then he will probably come back in the gloomy and foggy world in about one thousand years.

Katharine Trowbridge AGE 10 UNITED STATES

Time is a lonely worker resting on the millions of points in space. Passing at a steady pace. Never stopping. Noiseless.

Rick Rothenberg AGE 10 UNITED STATES

Life is life and no one can break it cause the world never ends because when people die another gets born so that is why I say that.

Anne Sargent AGE 6 CANADA

AT THE EDGE

When you come to the edge you *think* you have come to the end—but you've only come to part of the beginning, the beginning is the start for anyone, you will never come to the end, but keep on going.

John R. Sullivan AGE 8 UNITED STATES

[*Acknowledgments continued from copyright page*]

member when I got mad," copyright © 1969 by Ernie Rubinstein.

"Life is Life," copyright © 1969 by Anne Sargent.

"On a Foggy Morning," copyright © 1969 by Karen Saunders.

"Blindness," copyright © 1969 by Lori Schectman.

"A flower feels like feathers," and "It is awful," copyright © 1969 by Amy Schwartz.

"My pretend friend," copyright © 1969 by Harry Schneider.

"There are two worlds," and "When I get angry," copyright © 1969 by George Semper.

"When I Was Three Years Old," and "The Scary Doll," copyright © 1969 by Robin Shakelford.

"The Cup of Tea," and "The Incinerator," copyright © 1969 by Christine Short.

"The Adventures of a Toy," copyright © 1969 by David Solomon.

"Of All the Strange People I Have Met," copyright © 1969 by David Spiro.

"It," copyright © 1969 by Virginia Staples.

"The earth voomed out," copyright © 1969 by Adam Sternglass.

"My Goat Tinker Bell," and "Fear," copyright © 1969 by Susan Streeter.

"At the Edge," copyright © 1969 by John R. Sullivan.

"The duck likes to blow balloons up," copyright © 1969 by Rachel Tannenbaum.

"My Irritation," copyright © 1969 by Sandie Thorkildson, appeared in *Anthology 1962–1963* and is used with the permission of Minneapolis Area Council of Teachers of English.

"I am a person," and "A person walking in black boots," copyright © 1969 by Katharine Trowbridge.

"Sometimes when you meet your relatives," copyright © 1969 by Paul Uhlir.

"To touch an old person's hand," and "Dying," copyright © 1969 by David Urrows.

"Charlie," copyright © 1969 by John Van Gordon.

"The Theater," copyright © 1969 by Geoffrey Waghorn.

"My Own River Bank," copyright © 1969 by Scott Welke.

"The Dragon That Could Not Breathe Fire," copyright © 1969 by Jacqueline Weller.

"Love," copyright © 1969 by David Wilson.

"The Darkness," copyright © 1969 by Ian Wilson.

"When I Saw a Wreck," copyright © 1969 by Lawther Wood.

"Tulips," "Cave Men," and "One day when I came home I started to act daft" are used with the permission of the County Council of West Riding and Chatto & Windus Ltd., and originally appeared in *The Excitement of Writing,* edited by A. B. Clegg.

"Quiet Fishing," by Michael Freeman and "The Wave," are used with the permission of Mr. J. E. H. Blackie.

"Me," and "My Brother," by David Deakon, "The Nightmare," by Jacqueline Lesly Wright, "A Game of Dentists," by Simon Mark Abbey, "The Giant," by Jeremy Roberts, "Class 1 had Monday off," by Sally-Anne Fryman and "Noise," by Elizabeth Mary Watson first appeared in *Children as Writers* and are used with the permission of The Daily Mirror Newspapers Limited.

"The Fox," copyright © 1969 by Alexander McNeil, and "My House on 18th Street," copyright © 1969 by Carolyn Patterson, are used with the permission of The New Thing Art and Architecture Center, Washington, D.C.

"Playing Soccer," by Tommy Waldie; "Chewing Gum," by Graeme S.; "Song of the Cricket," by Marilyn; and "Grandpop Picking Flowers," by Queenie Davies are used with the permission of Elwyn Richardson.

"Planet Z," copyright © 1969 by Michael Olenick; "My Friend," and "Richie's Friend," copyright © 1969 by Ianta Washington; "How Stupid I Am," copyright © 1969 by Enid Talbert, used with the permission of *Muse,* Bedford Lincoln Neighborhood Museum in Bedford Stuyvesant, Brooklyn, New York, and Kenneth Koch, director of the writing workshop, and instructors Philip Lopate and Bill Wortheim.

I would like to thank the teachers and organizations who generously supplied the illustrations by children. A list of artists and sources follows:

Title page. "Natives Hunting Buffalo, by Kenneth Foulner, age 8, used with the permission of the London *Daily Mirror.*

Page 6. "Sturminster Carnival Procession." by Robert Cowly, age 9, used with the permission of the London *Daily Mirror.*

Page 13. "Summer Flower," by Suke, age 7, Horizon's Edge School, Canterbury, New Hampshire.

Page 27. "The Fun Boat," by Paul, age 13, Horizon's Edge School, Canterbury, New Hampshire.

Page 55. "Thomas, My Cat," by Janet, age 10, Horizon's Edge School, Canterbury, New Hampshire.

Page 73. By a child age 7, Manhattan Country School, New York.

Page 101. By D. Marshall, age 10, Pocklington School, England.

Page 129. By Clara Jean Kaskinen, age 11, Auer Avenue School, Milwaukee, Wisconsin.

Page 149. By Peter Zucker, age 8, Manhattan Country School, New York.

Page 179. "Spook Tree," by Marien, age 7, Horizon's Edge School, Canterbury, New Hampshire.

Page 195. By Emile Svitzer, age 8, Manhattan Country School, New York.